Watch Me Read and Draw

The Zoo

By Samantha Chagollan

Illustrated by Mattia Cerato

How to Use This Book

This book is special because it blends two things together that kids love. In this book, you get to read AND draw!
Inside, you will find:

A fun story to read

11 step-by-step drawing lessons

A flip-out drawing pad with guidelines

Stickers to complete each scene

A scene to make your own

Swinging through the trees to the next habitat, Liam stops in to see his friend the giraffe. "Have you seen the toucan?" he asks, but she shakes her tall head. "Check next door!" she shouts after him as he swings away.

Draw the giraffe!

1 2 3 4 5 6

When you finish your drawing, place the carrots sticker on the opposite page!

Draw the giraffe's tail, her ears, and her horns. Add her mane, spotted pattern, face, and hooves.

Draw your own scene with your favorite zoo animals here, and add some stickers too!

Here is the best way to enjoy this book:
Sit down with an adult and grab
your drawing and coloring supplies.

Read through the story together,
following along with each lesson
on the flip-out drawing pad.

Draw the giraffe's tail, her ears, and her horns.
Add her mane, spotted pattern, face, and hooves.

Swinging through the trees to the next habitat, Liam
stops in to see his friend the giraffe. "Have you seen the
toucan?" he asks, but she shakes her tall head.
"Check next door!" she shouts after him
as he swings away.

When you complete a
lesson, add a sticker to
the scene. Good job!

Draw your own scene with your favorite zoo animals here,
and add some stickers too!

Draw your own scene at
the end with the characters
you have learned, and add
some stickers.

**Great work! Now you can draw these
zoo animals any time you want!**

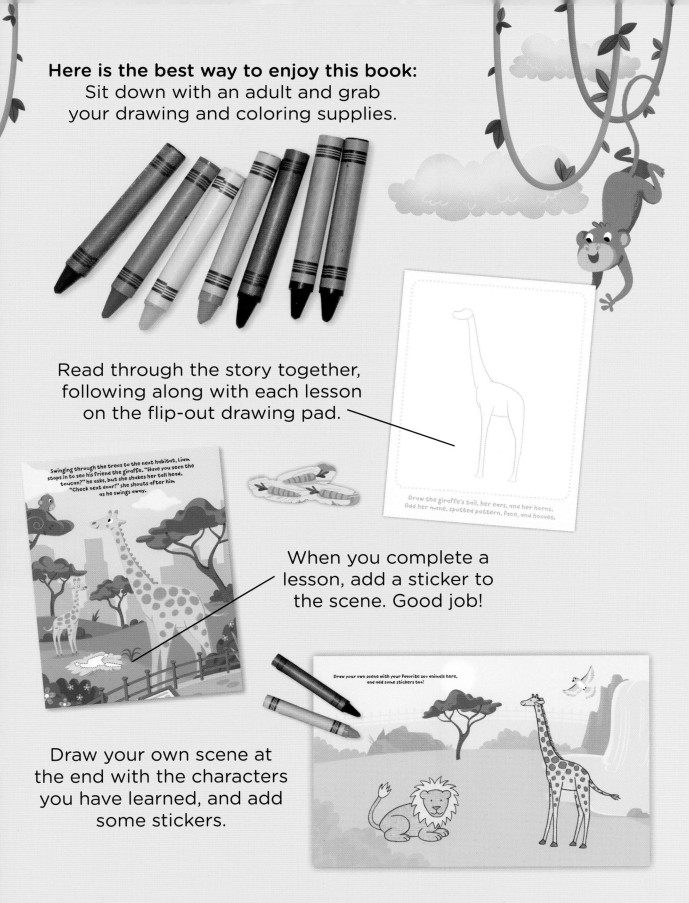

The sun is shining at the Zoo, and Liam the monkey is just settling into his favorite tree when he happens to overhear something curious. "Can you believe it?" says one zookeeper to the other, "The toucan seems to have disappeared!"

Liam is not the kind of monkey to sit around while a mystery is waiting to be solved! He decides to set out on a mission to find the missing toucan, and bring him back home.

Draw the monkey!

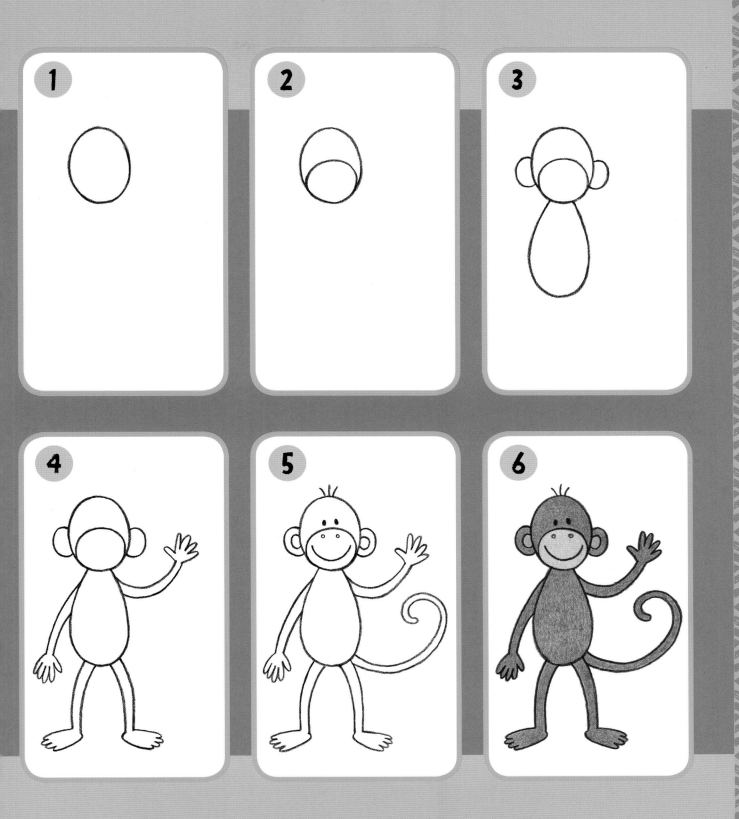

When you finish your drawing, place the
monkey sticker on the opposite page!

Just outside of the monkey habitat, Liam sees a crowd gathering around a sign. "Where could he be?" the visitors ask each other.

Draw the toucan!

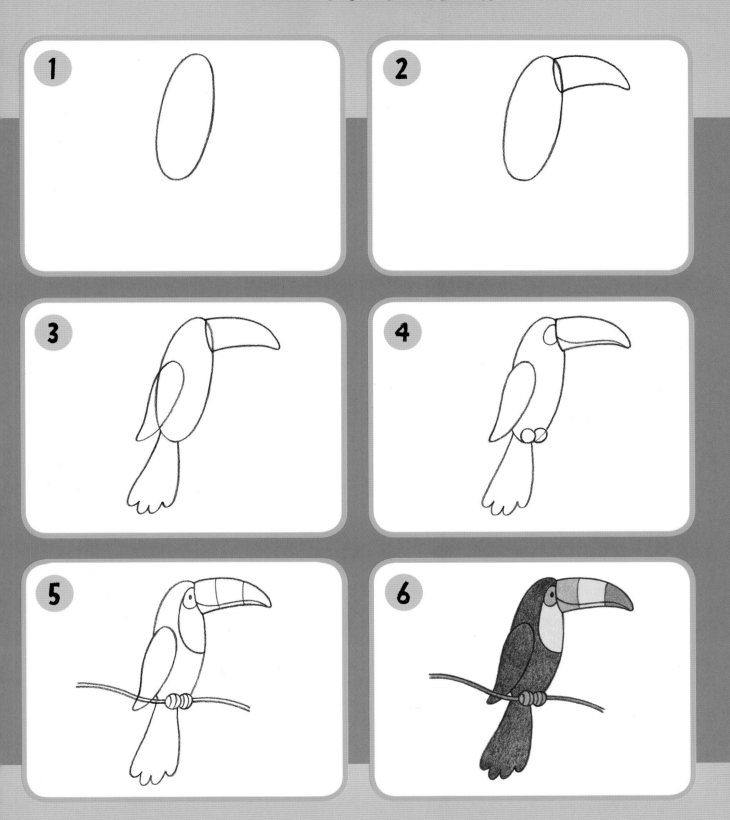

When you finish your drawing, place the camera sticker on the opposite page!

Liam decides to start his search nearby. He hops over to his next-door neighbor the panda bear. "Have you seen the toucan?" he asks, but the panda bear is chewing a mouthful of bamboo leaves and doesn't reply.

Draw the panda bear!

When you finish your drawing, place the
fish sticker on the opposite page!

Swinging through the trees to the next habitat, Liam stops in to see his friend the giraffe. "Have you seen the toucan?" he asks, but she shakes her tall head. "Check next door!" she shouts after him as he swings away.

Draw the giraffe!

When you finish your drawing, place the
carrots sticker on the opposite page!

The zebra is happy to see Liam, and asks if he wants to play a game of hide and seek. "I can't," says Liam. "Have you seen the toucan?"
"Yes!" says the zebra. "I think he wanted to ask the elephant for some advice."

Draw the zebra!

When you finish your drawing, place the
bird sticker on the opposite page!

"Hey you guys," yells Liam over the elephants' loud trumpeting sounds. "Where's the toucan?"
"We haven't seen him since yesterday," says the smallest elephant.
"He flew that way!"

Draw the elephant!

When you finish your drawing, place the
monkey sticker on the opposite page!

Hot on the trail of this new clue, Liam scampers over to the hippo's pond. She is too busy playing in the mud to answer his questions!

Draw the hippo!

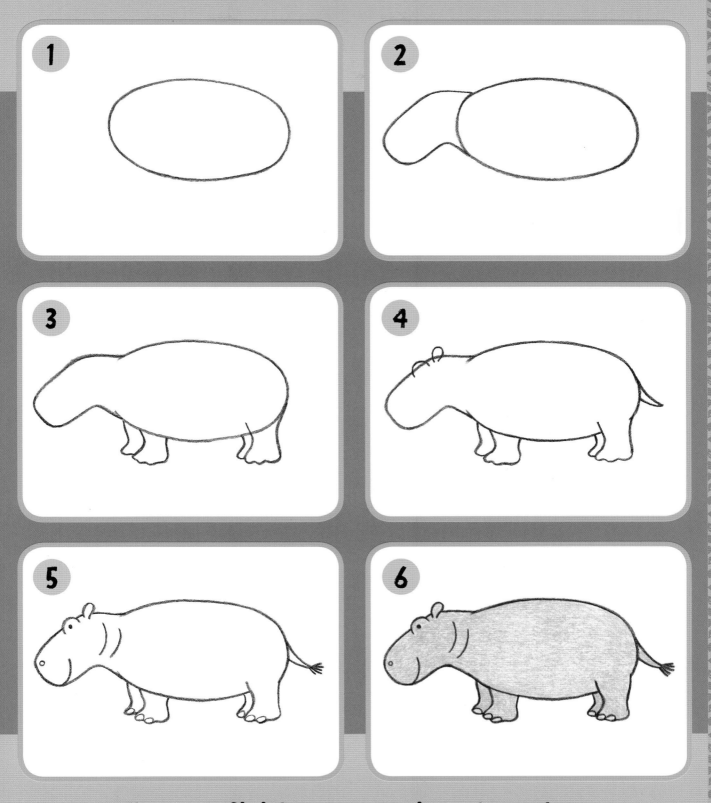

When you finish your drawing, place the
baby hippo sticker on the opposite page!

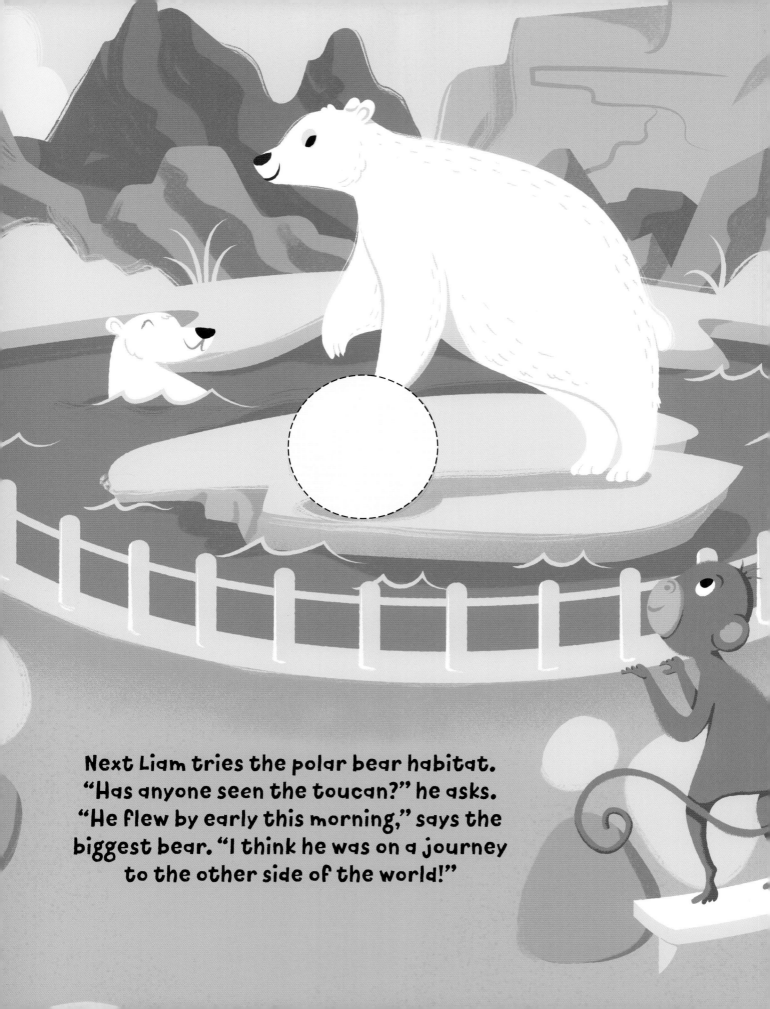

Next Liam tries the polar bear habitat.
"Has anyone seen the toucan?" he asks.
"He flew by early this morning," says the
biggest bear. "I think he was on a journey
to the other side of the world!"

Draw the polar bear!

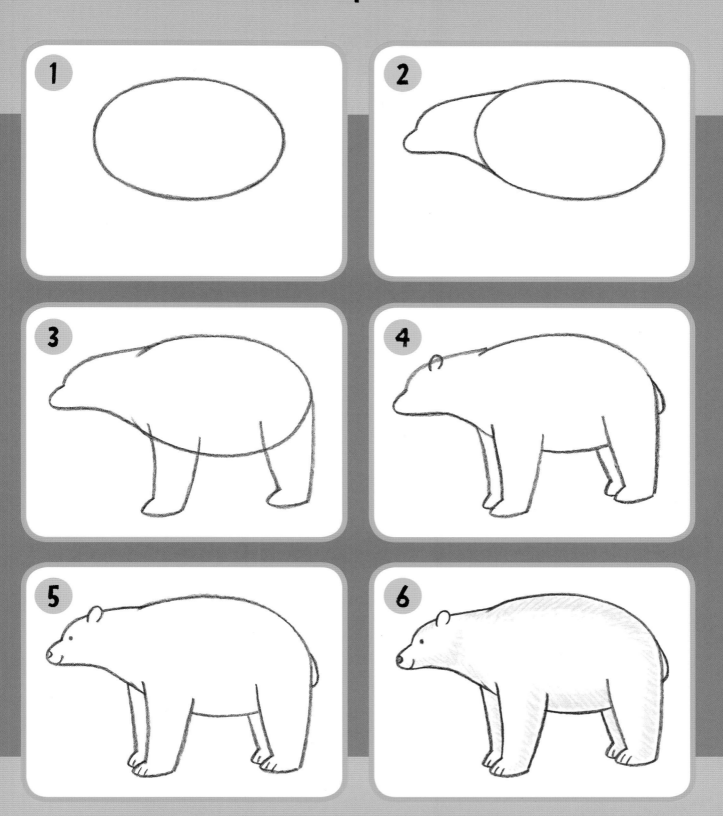

When you finish your drawing, place the
ball sticker on the opposite page!

The arctic habitat is all the way on the other side of the zoo. The toucan has to be there! Liam scurries as fast as he can through the park, and finally finds the penguins. "Where is the toucan?" he asks. One points left with a shiny flipper.

Draw the penguin!

When you finish your drawing, place the
penguin sticker on the opposite page!

Liam follows the penguin's directions and comes to
the eucalyptus trees, where the koalas live.
"Have you seen the toucan?" he asks.
"Yes, he was just here," says a baby koala.
"But he was hungry!"

Draw the koala bear!

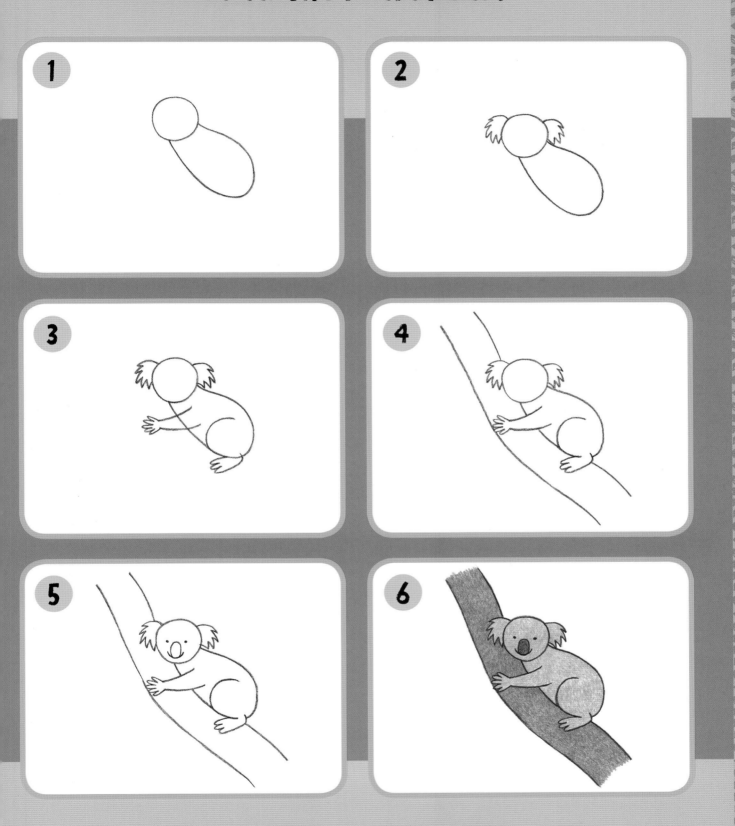

When you finish your drawing, place the
koala sticker on the opposite page!

Liam knows that toucans love guavas, and the only guava trees in the zoo are in the lion habitat. Hurry, Liam! He arrives just in time to see the toucan snacking on a juicy guava. With the toucan mystery solved, everyone can go back to enjoying a beautiful day at the zoo!

Draw the lion!

When you finish your drawing, place the
butterfly sticker on the opposite page!

The End

Draw your own scene with your favorite zoo animals here,
and add some stickers too!

Great job!

_____

Print your name here

Congratulations on completing the story. Keep drawing and reading!

Finish-the-Scene Stickers